PLAYING OUD

A Complete Beginner-to-Advanced Guide to Oud Techniques, Tuning, Finger Placement, Maqam Theory, Improvisation, and Traditional Middle Eastern Music Mastery

Garcia Blau

Copyright © 2025 By Garcia Blau

All Right Reserved

No portion of this work may be copied, stored, or shared in any format—whether electronic, mechanical, photographic, recorded, or otherwise—without the author's prior written consent, except for short excerpts used in reviews, academic analysis, or other legally permitted fair use cases.

All rights are reserved by the author. For permission requests, licensing inquiries, or any concerns regarding usage rights, please contact the author in writing. Unauthorized use, reproduction, or distribution is strictly prohibited and may result in legal action under applicable copyright laws.

Published by Garcia Blau

Disclaimer

This book is intended as a general guide to learning and playing musical instruments. While the techniques and insights provided can support skill development, they do not replace personalized instruction from a qualified music teacher. Individual progress will vary based on practice, experience, and proper application of techniques.

The author and publisher make no guarantees regarding the accuracy, completeness, or suitability of the material for every learner. As music education continues to evolve, some methods or recommendations may not reflect the latest research or teaching approaches. For tailored guidance based on your specific goals, challenges, or physical needs, consulting a professional instructor is strongly advised.

Safety and Responsibility

Proper posture, instrument care, and correct technique are essential to prevent injury and ensure effective learning. Always follow safety guidelines provided by certified instructors.

The author and publisher disclaim any liability for injury, damage, or loss—including harm to individuals, instruments, or property—resulting from the use or misuse of this book's content.

By using this material, you accept full responsibility for your learning experience and commit to practicing safely and mindfully.

Table of Contents

WHAT THIS BOOK OFFER 10

CHAPTER ONE 13

   Introduction 13

      Brief History of the Oud and Its Cultural Significance 14

      The Importance of Mastering Traditional Techniques for Success in Oud Playing 16

      How Oud Playing Connects to Music and Business 18

      Overview of How This Guide Will Assist Beginners in Becoming Skilled Players and Successful Musicians 20

      Tips for Getting the Most Out of Your Learning Experience 22

CHAPTER TWO 25

   Getting Started with the Oud 25

      Basic Introduction to the Oud Instrument and Its Parts 26

      How to Choose the Right Oud for Beginners 28

      Proper Care and Maintenance of Your Oud 30

      First Steps in Learning: Tuning Your Oud .. 32

      Easy-to-Follow Exercises to Get Comfortable with the Instrument 35

CHAPTER THREE 39

Understanding Traditional Oud Techniques ... 39

- The Importance of Finger Placement and Hand Posture 41
- How to Properly Use the Pick (Risha) 43
- Basic Strumming and Plucking Techniques 44
- Introduction to Different Oud Scales and Modes 47
- Building Your First Simple Oud Melodies ... 49

CHAPTER FOUR 51

Mastering the Essential Oud Skills 51

- Advanced Techniques: Tremolo, Sliding, and Ornamentation 53
- 1. Tremolo: Creating Rich, Sustained Sounds 54
- 2. Sliding: Smooth Transitions Between Notes 54
- 3. Ornamentation: Adding Subtle Flourishes 55
- Practice Tips for Improving Finger Dexterity and Speed 56
- 1. Slow and Steady Wins the Race 56
- 2. Finger Independence Exercises 57
- 3. Focus on Left-Hand Movement 57
- 4. Alternate Picking for Speed 58

Developing a Strong Sense of Rhythm and Timing 58

1. Understanding the Rhythmic Structure ... 59

2. Playing with a Metronome 59

3. Playing Along with Other Musicians 60

Understanding Oud Notation and Music Theory Basics 60

1. Oud Tuning and Scales 61

2. Learning Intervals and Chords 61

3. Sight-Reading and Notation 62

Exercises for Improving Your Playing Speed and Accuracy 62

1. Chromatic Scales 63

2. Arpeggio Patterns 63

3. Double Stops and Trills 63

CHAPTER FIVE 65

Turning Your Oud Passion into a Profitable Business 65

Identifying Opportunities for Profit Through Oud Playing 66

Building an Online Presence for Your Music Business 69

How to Create a Professional Portfolio as an Oud Musician 71

Monetizing Your Skills: Teaching, Performing, and Recording 74

Networking Tips and How to Grow Your Business Locally and Globally 76

CHAPTER SIX 79

Common Challenges and How to Overcome Them 79

1. Difficulty in Mastering Finger Techniques and Overcoming Hand Fatigue 80

2. How to Deal with Slow Progress and Stay Motivated 82

3. Common Mistakes in Playing and How to Correct Them 84

4. Finding the Right Resources and Learning Tools 86

5. Dealing with Performance Anxiety and Gaining Confidence on Stage 89

CHAPTER SEVEN 93

Long-Term Success in Oud Playing and Business 93

Setting Long-Term Goals for Your Musical and Business Growth 94

Continuous Improvement: Ongoing Practice and Education 95

How to Evolve Your Unique Style as an Oud Player 97

Building a Loyal Fan Base and Growing Your Audience 99

Sustainable Ways to Make a Career in Music with Oud Playing 101

Conclusion: The Path to Mastery and Profit.104

Reflecting on Your Progress and Future Goals in Oud Playing 105

The Importance of Persistence and Dedication in Both Music and Business....107

How to Stay Connected with the Oud Community and Continue Learning 109

Encouragement to Pursue Your Passion and Turn It Into a Successful Career 110

Final Words of Motivation to Keep Going on Your Journey of Mastery..........................112

THE END 114

WHAT THIS BOOK OFFER

"Playing Oud" is an essential guide for anyone eager to explore the world of this ancient and soulful instrument. Whether you're a beginner or someone with a bit of experience, this book is designed to take you through the necessary steps to master Oud playing while understanding its profound cultural significance. From the very first chapter, readers are introduced to the history of the Oud, which traces its roots through centuries of rich musical tradition. This not only deepens your appreciation for the instrument but also connects you to a broader cultural heritage that has shaped music across the world.

The importance of mastering traditional techniques is emphasized throughout this book. Oud playing isn't just about strumming notes; it's about understanding the intricate hand posture, finger placements, and how to use the pick (Risha) effectively. This foundation is crucial for success in Oud playing, and this book ensures that you're well-equipped to master these essential skills early on. Each section guides you step-by-step with easy-to-follow exercises, offering an accessible approach for beginners. Whether tuning your instrument or learning your first melody, the book's practical approach helps you make immediate progress.

What sets this guide apart is its focus on connecting music with business. "Playing Oud" doesn't simply teach you how to play the instrument; it also helps you turn your passion into a profitable career. This book explores ways to identify opportunities within the music industry, including how to establish a strong online presence, create a professional portfolio, and even monetize your skills through teaching, performing, and recording. By emphasizing networking and personal branding, this guide gives you the tools needed to grow your music business both locally and globally.

As you dive deeper into this book, you'll learn advanced techniques such as tremolo, sliding, and ornamentation, helping you refine your skills and develop a unique musical style. But it doesn't shy away from the challenges that come with learning an intricate instrument like the Oud. From overcoming hand fatigue to dealing with performance anxiety, this book offers practical advice on how to stay motivated and push through the difficult moments. This makes it not just a musical guide, but also a supportive resource for personal growth and resilience.

CHAPTER ONE
Introduction

The Oud, often referred to as the "King of Instruments" in the Middle Eastern music tradition, carries with it a rich history and a profound cultural significance. Learning to play the Oud not only opens the door to a deeper understanding of music from the Arab world, but it also provides a pathway for personal growth and artistic development. Whether you're drawn to the warm, rich tones of the Oud or the challenge of mastering its unique techniques, your journey in learning this ancient instrument will be a transformative one.

This guide is designed to provide you with a structured approach to learning Oud, with a focus on both musical proficiency and career development. As a beginner, you may feel overwhelmed by the complexity of the instrument, but with patience, dedication, and the right guidance, you can become a skilled player. Moreover, mastering the Oud can provide opportunities for success not only in music but also in the broader business world. Understanding the connection between artistry and entrepreneurship will be a central theme throughout this guide.

By focusing on traditional techniques and offering expert advice, this guide will help you maximize your learning experience, refine your technique, and prepare you for a successful career as an Oud musician.

Brief History of the Oud and Its Cultural Significance

The Oud has a history that spans thousands of years, with its origins traced back to the ancient civilizations of Mesopotamia, Persia, and Egypt. Its design is believed to have been inspired by earlier stringed instruments such as the Greek *barbitos* and the Persian *lute*. Over the centuries, the Oud evolved into the instrument we recognize today, becoming a staple in Middle Eastern, North African, and Mediterranean music.

In terms of cultural significance, the Oud holds a special place in Arab music and is often seen as a symbol of the region's artistic and intellectual legacy. It has been used to accompany poets, tell stories, and evoke emotions in listeners. The instrument is integral to classical Arab music ensembles, as well as modern interpretations of traditional sounds.

The sound of the Oud is deeply intertwined with the cultural fabric of the Middle East. It has the power to connect listeners with ancient traditions, conveying everything from joy to sorrow, and providing an emotional outlet for musicians. This instrument is often seen not only as a means of musical expression but also as a way to preserve and share the history of a people and their heritage.

Understanding the historical and cultural context of the Oud is essential to mastering the instrument, as it allows you to approach your playing with a deeper sense of respect and connection to its roots.

The Importance of Mastering Traditional Techniques for Success in Oud Playing

Mastering traditional techniques is key to becoming a proficient Oud player and ensuring the authenticity of your music. Unlike many other instruments, the Oud requires a highly nuanced approach to both technique and expression. Traditional playing techniques such as *pizzicato* (plucking with the fingers), *tremolo* (rapid plucking for sustained notes), and *vibrato* (subtle pitch variation) are fundamental to achieving the characteristic sound of the Oud.

One of the most challenging aspects of playing the Oud is developing control over the string tension and plucking technique, which directly affects the tone and resonance of the instrument. The delicate balance between the right hand's strumming or plucking and the left hand's finger positioning is essential for producing clean and beautiful notes.

Additionally, understanding the Arabic *maqamat* (musical modes) is a crucial aspect of Oud playing. These scales are vastly different from Western scales, incorporating microtones that give the music a distinct flavor. Mastering the intricacies of these modes allows players to express a wide range of emotions and is central to playing Oud in an authentic, culturally respectful way.

Committing to mastering these traditional techniques will not only elevate your playing but also honor the centuries of music that have come before you. It is essential to spend time learning the techniques of the great Oud masters, as their skills and methods will serve as your foundation for success.

How Oud Playing Connects to Music and Business

In today's globalized world, the boundaries between music and business have become increasingly blurred. While the Oud is a traditional instrument, learning it opens up many professional opportunities, both in the music world and beyond. As a musician, understanding how to turn your passion for Oud playing into a sustainable career requires more than just technical proficiency—it also requires a keen awareness of the business side of music.

One of the most prominent ways Oud players can succeed in business is by embracing the role of cultural ambassador. As Middle Eastern music gains recognition around the world, skilled Oud players are in high demand for performances, collaborations, and music festivals. You can build a career by leveraging your unique sound to reach audiences both locally and internationally.

In addition to performance, there are other avenues where Oud playing intersects with business. Teaching is another avenue for musicians to create a steady income stream, especially if you position yourself as an expert in traditional music or offer private lessons. Furthermore, recording your music, creating instructional content, and even developing your own brand as an Oud musician can help you expand your business prospects.

In today's digital age, platforms like YouTube, Spotify, and Instagram offer unprecedented opportunities for musicians to showcase their talent. For an Oud player, utilizing social media to create an online presence is crucial in expanding reach and finding new business opportunities.

Mastering the instrument and understanding the intersection of music and business will empower you to succeed in your musical career and potentially create lasting financial success.

Overview of How This Guide Will Assist Beginners in Becoming Skilled Players and Successful Musicians

This guide is specifically designed for beginners who are eager to start their journey with the Oud. We understand the challenges of beginning with an instrument that has a rich history and unique playing techniques, which is why this guide is structured to help you every step of the way.

We begin with the basics—introducing you to the Oud's anatomy, how to tune it, and how to properly hold the instrument. Then, we dive into essential techniques, such as finger placement, plucking methods, and understanding the concept of *maqamat*. As you progress, we introduce you to playing simple tunes, gradually building up your skills.

To make the learning experience more engaging, we offer a variety of exercises and practical tips that encourage regular practice and improvement.

Importantly, this guide does not stop at technical skills. We also delve into the mindset and discipline needed for consistent practice. We help you understand how to approach music with patience and an open mind, making the process of learning the Oud both enjoyable and fulfilling.

As you advance, we offer advice on performance, creative expression, and even how to manage your career as an Oud musician. Whether you aspire to be a solo performer, a collaborator, or a music teacher, this guide will provide the resources you need to turn your passion for Oud playing into a successful and meaningful career.

Tips for Getting the Most Out of Your Learning Experience

To get the most out of your Oud learning journey, it's important to approach your practice sessions with intention and dedication. Here are some tips that will help you maximize your learning experience:

1. **Consistency is Key** – Set aside time each day for practice. Even 20 minutes a day can make a significant difference in your progress.
2. **Focus on Technique** – While it's tempting to jump into playing songs, remember that proper technique is the foundation of great playing. Spend time focusing on finger placement, strumming techniques, and the intricacies of the *maqamat*.
3. **Listen to Master Players** – Learning from the masters is invaluable. Listen to

recordings of renowned Oud musicians and try to replicate their techniques and sounds.

4. **Record Yourself** – Listening to recordings of your own playing helps you identify areas for improvement that might be hard to hear in the moment.

5. **Join a Community** – Whether it's online or in person, connecting with fellow Oud players can provide inspiration, support, and opportunities for collaboration.

6. **Stay Open to Experimentation** – While learning traditional techniques is important, don't be afraid to experiment and inject your own style into your playing. The beauty of music lies in personal expression.

By following these tips and remaining dedicated to your practice, you'll not only become a skilled Oud player but also lay the groundwork for a successful and fulfilling musical career.

CHAPTER TWO
Getting Started with the Oud

The Oud is a beautiful, traditional stringed instrument that has been the heartbeat of Middle Eastern music for centuries. It is a key component of various musical genres, offering a distinct and resonant sound. Whether you are a complete beginner or someone who has been interested in playing the Oud for a while, understanding its history, components, and techniques is essential. This guide will take you through the first steps of your Oud journey, from choosing the right instrument to mastering basic tuning and playing exercises.

Basic Introduction to the Oud Instrument and Its Parts

The Oud is a fretless, pear-shaped instrument known for its warm, deep sound. It has a rich cultural heritage and is often seen as the precursor to the European lute. Here's a breakdown of the main parts of the Oud:

- **Body**: The body of the Oud is large and pear-shaped, crafted from wood, typically made of rosewood or walnut. This part is the resonating chamber that gives the instrument its deep, mellow tones.
- **Soundboard (Top)**: The top of the Oud is usually made of spruce or cedar and is vital for sound production. It is slightly arched and is perforated with sound holes, often shaped like rosettes, to enhance resonance.
- **Neck**: The neck is long and slender, with no frets, allowing for a wide range of pitches.

This is where you'll spend most of your time when playing, as it holds the fingerboard.
- **Strings**: The Oud typically has 11 or 13 strings, grouped into 5 or 6 courses. These strings are tuned in pairs, and the instrument's tuning and the interplay of these strings produce its rich sound.
- **Bridge**: The bridge is where the strings are attached to the body of the Oud. It plays a crucial role in transmitting the vibrations of the strings to the soundboard.
- **Pegs**: The pegs are located at the top of the neck and are used to adjust the tension of the strings for tuning.

Learning the Oud is a rewarding experience, but it's important to familiarize yourself with these parts before you start. Each component works together to create the unmistakable sound of the Oud.

How to Choose the Right Oud for Beginners

Selecting the right Oud can be a challenge, especially if you are new to the instrument. There are several factors you need to consider to ensure you purchase a quality instrument that suits your needs.

1. Type of Oud

Ouds come in various types and sizes. While the classic Arabic Oud is the most popular, there are also Turkish and Persian Ouds, each with slight differences in sound and structure. Beginners are usually advised to start with an Arabic Oud, as it offers a balance of tone and versatility.

2. Material Quality

The material used in the construction of the Oud is one of the most important factors affecting its sound quality. A well-made Oud should have a solid wood body, a high-quality soundboard, and a durable neck. Avoid Ouds made from plastic or other low-quality materials as these will not produce a pleasing sound.

3. Size

Ouds come in different sizes, so it's important to select one that feels comfortable. Beginners should aim for a standard size that is easy to handle. If you are a child or have smaller hands, consider looking for a smaller-sized Oud designed for young players.

4. Price

As with any musical instrument, the price range of Ouds can vary. While high-end, handcrafted models are often expensive, there are also well-made beginner models that don't break the bank. It's crucial to find an Oud that fits your budget while still offering quality sound and construction.

5. Playability

Before purchasing an Oud, try it out if possible. Ensure the strings are not too high off the neck (which could make it difficult to play), and that the instrument is in good condition. If buying online, check reviews and ensure the seller offers a return policy in case you are unsatisfied.

Proper Care and Maintenance of Your Oud

Taking care of your Oud is essential to maintain its beautiful sound and longevity. Here are some essential care and maintenance tips:

1. Keep It Clean

Regularly clean your Oud to prevent dust, oil, and dirt from accumulating. Use a soft, dry cloth to wipe down the body, neck, and strings after each playing session. Avoid using harsh chemicals, as they can damage the wood or finish.

2. Humidity Control

Wooden instruments like the Oud are sensitive to changes in humidity. Too much humidity can cause the wood to swell, while too little can cause it to crack. Ideally, store your Oud in a room with moderate humidity. If you live in a dry area, consider using a humidifier or a humidity control pouch for the case.

3. String Maintenance

Oud strings are delicate and need to be replaced regularly to ensure optimal sound quality. Keep an eye on the condition of your strings and replace them when they start to sound dull or fray. Also, be sure to tune your Oud before each practice session.

4. Proper Storage

When not in use, store your Oud in its case to protect it from dust, humidity, and accidental damage. Always place the instrument in a safe, dry place, away from direct sunlight or extreme temperatures.

5. Regular Check-ups

As with any musical instrument, regular check-ups are important to ensure that the Oud remains in good playing condition. If you notice any issues such as buzzing or poor intonation, consider taking it to a professional for an inspection or repair.

First Steps in Learning: Tuning Your Oud

Before you start playing, it's important to properly tune your Oud. Tuning can seem daunting at first, but once you get the hang of it, it will become second nature.

1. Standard Tuning for the Oud

The standard tuning for a traditional Arabic Oud is usually as follows:

- **1st string (highest pitch): C**
- **2nd string: G**
- **3rd string: D**
- **4th string: A**
- **5th string: F**
- **6th string (lowest pitch): C**

These are the basic notes for each pair of strings (courses). Some variations exist based on personal preference or regional differences, so it's always a good idea to check with a teacher or reference materials for the tuning that best suits your style.

2. Using a Tuner

To begin tuning, use a clip-on tuner or a smartphone app designed for tuning instruments. Clip the tuner to the headstock of your Oud, and pluck each string individually. Adjust the pegs until the tuner shows the correct note for each string.

3. Tune the Strings in Pairs

Unlike many other stringed instruments, the Oud strings are usually tuned in pairs. Make sure that both strings in each course are tuned to the same pitch. You'll want the strings to ring together harmoniously.

4. Regular Tuning

It's essential to tune your Oud every time you play, as the strings tend to go out of tune due to changes in temperature and humidity. Consistent tuning helps to maintain the quality of sound and prevents undue strain on the strings.

Easy-to-Follow Exercises to Get Comfortable with the Instrument

Starting your practice with simple exercises will help you get comfortable with the Oud. Here are some beginner-friendly exercises to get you started:

1. Plucking and Strumming Exercises

Start by practicing basic plucking (using your right hand) and strumming motions. Try alternating between plucking each string with your thumb or plectrum (pick) and strumming the strings in a down-up motion. This will help build your right-hand coordination.

2. Simple Finger Exercises

To get used to the neck of the Oud and improve finger strength, try simple finger exercises like playing single notes on each string. Begin slowly and gradually build speed as you get more comfortable.

3. Simple Scales

Start learning basic scales, such as the C major scale. Play each note slowly, making sure your fingers are pressing down firmly and the notes are clear. This will help with intonation and finger placement.

4. Playing Simple Melodies

Once you've gotten comfortable with scales, try playing simple melodies. Many popular Middle Eastern songs have repetitive and easy-to-follow melodies that you can practice. This will help improve your ability to pick up tunes by ear.

5. Consistency is Key

Remember that learning an instrument is a gradual process. Practicing regularly, even for short periods, will lead to steady improvement. Be patient and enjoy the journey of learning your Oud!

By following these foundational steps, you will have the tools you need to get started with the Oud. With practice and dedication, you'll soon be playing beautiful music on this extraordinary instrument.

CHAPTER THREE
Understanding Traditional Oud Techniques

The Oud, often referred to as the "king of instruments" in the Arab world, holds a prestigious position in Middle Eastern music. Mastering the Oud involves an in-depth understanding of its history, cultural significance, and traditional techniques. These techniques have been passed down through generations, from skilled artisans to passionate musicians. The Oud is unique in that it's not just an instrument—it's a connection to centuries of musical tradition.

The traditional techniques of playing the Oud require more than just technical ability—they require a deep respect for the instrument and its rich cultural roots. When learning these techniques, it is essential to start by familiarizing oneself with the anatomy of the Oud. The Oud is a stringed instrument with a pear-shaped body and no frets, allowing for an expressive, nuanced sound. The absence of frets means the player must rely on finger placement and precise tuning to produce the desired notes.

There are several traditional styles of playing the Oud, each representing a specific region or period. The classical Arabic style, for example, focuses on creating rich melodic lines, while Turkish Oud playing tends to emphasize rapid, intricate finger movements. Regardless of the style, all Oud players must maintain strong control over the rhythm and expression, as the Oud is a deeply emotional instrument.

The Importance of Finger Placement and Hand Posture

When playing the Oud, finger placement and hand posture are absolutely critical to producing the correct sound and avoiding strain. Unlike instruments with frets, such as the guitar, the Oud demands a heightened level of finger precision. Every note is determined by how and where you press the strings against the fingerboard, making finger placement one of the first areas that require attention from beginners.

Proper finger placement involves pressing the strings down firmly but not too hard, ensuring that the sound produced is clear and resonant. The fingers should be placed close to the frets without touching them, as this allows the string to vibrate freely. For beginners, this might take some practice, as pressing the strings too lightly can result in a dull sound, while pressing them too hard can cause unwanted buzzing or muted notes.

Hand posture also plays a crucial role in playing the Oud effectively. The left hand, which is responsible for pressing the strings, should maintain a relaxed and natural position. A stiff or tense hand can result in finger fatigue and affect your ability to play fluidly. Meanwhile, the right hand, which holds the pick (Risha), should maintain a loose and flexible wrist. Keeping the wrist relaxed helps in producing smooth, rhythmic strokes while preventing strain.

It's also important to keep both hands aligned with the body of the instrument. The left hand should always hover close to the neck, avoiding unnecessary stretches, and the right hand should move freely across the strings without locking the wrist. These subtle details, while simple, can have a significant impact on the quality of sound and your overall playing comfort.

How to Properly Use the Pick (Risha)

The pick, or Risha, is an essential component in Oud playing. Unlike guitar picks, the Risha is traditionally made from feathers or plastic, and it has a unique shape designed for producing a deep, resonant tone. The way you hold and use the Risha can completely change the sound of your playing, so mastering this technique is vital.

When holding the Risha, the fingers of the right hand should grasp it loosely, with the index and thumb providing support while the rest of the fingers rest naturally around it. The Risha should not be gripped too tightly, as this can cause stiffness and a loss of fluidity in your playing. The right wrist should remain relaxed to ensure smooth, fluid movements as you strike the strings.

Strumming or plucking the strings requires specific techniques depending on the musical style. For traditional Arabic music, a mix of down-strokes (from the bass to the treble strings) and up-strokes (from treble to bass) is common. The pick should be angled slightly when plucking the strings to achieve a clean, bright sound. Be mindful of the pressure you apply while strumming, as too much pressure can mute the sound, while too little can make the notes sound weak.

When practicing with the Risha, start slowly to ensure that you are producing clear, even sounds. Over time, your speed and control will increase, allowing you to incorporate more complex techniques, such as tremolo (rapid up and down strokes) or dynamic variations in your playing.

Basic Strumming and Plucking Techniques

Strumming and plucking are the foundation of playing the Oud. The instrument's unique design allows for a variety of strumming and plucking techniques that contribute to its distinctive sound.

There are two primary techniques to master: strumming and plucking.

Strumming: This is one of the most fundamental techniques for playing the Oud. When strumming, you move the Risha across all of the strings in a sweeping motion. To produce a balanced sound, the wrist should stay loose, and the movement should come from the forearm rather than the fingers. You can experiment with different strumming patterns, from the steady rhythm used in classical music to the more intricate, fast-paced patterns found in folk music.

For beginners, it's best to practice basic downstrokes (moving the Risha from the top strings to the lower ones) and upstrokes (moving from the lower strings back up). Once comfortable with these basic motions, you can begin to combine them in various sequences to create more complex patterns.

Plucking: Plucking is another essential technique, where each string is individually plucked with the Risha. This technique is crucial for creating melodies and is often used in solo performances. Plucking involves using the pick to strike individual strings in a controlled manner, creating a clean, distinct sound. To pluck effectively, it's important to ensure that your wrist remains relaxed, and your movements are precise.

Both strumming and plucking should be practiced slowly at first, ensuring that each note rings out clearly. Over time, you can increase the speed and complexity of your strumming and plucking patterns. The goal is to create a seamless flow between these two techniques, which will allow you to perform more advanced compositions with confidence and precision.

Introduction to Different Oud Scales and Modes

The Oud is played in a variety of scales and modes, many of which are distinct from Western music theory. These scales, called "maqamat" (plural of maqam), form the foundation of Middle Eastern music and give each piece its unique flavor and emotional impact. Understanding these scales is key to mastering the Oud and unlocking its full expressive potential.

Some of the most common Maqamat include:

- **Maqam Rast:** This is one of the most popular scales in Arabic music, often associated with feelings of joy and strength. It is similar to the Western major scale but with slight variations in intervals, giving it a more exotic flavor.
- **Maqam Bayati:** Known for its melancholic and contemplative nature, this scale is often used in slower, more reflective pieces. It has

a slightly lower third degree than the Western major scale, which imparts its unique sound.
- **Maqam Hijaz:** Often used in more dramatic or intense pieces, the Hijaz scale features a raised second and sixth degree, giving it a distinct, exotic quality.
- **Maqam Saba:** A particularly emotional scale that conveys sadness and longing, the Saba scale is characterized by its lowered second and sixth degrees.

Each maqam has its own set of rules for how it can be used melodically and harmonically, and learning these will allow you to play with more expressive depth. To begin, familiarize yourself with the intervals of each maqam and practice playing simple melodies within these scales. Once comfortable, try to incorporate more complex ornamentations, such as trills or slides, to bring the scales to life.

Building Your First Simple Oud Melodies

Now that you've learned the fundamental techniques and scales, it's time to start creating simple melodies on the Oud. Building a melody on the Oud can be a deeply satisfying experience, as you begin to see how the techniques you've learned come together to create beautiful music.

Start by selecting a maqam (scale) you feel comfortable with, such as Maqam Rast. Using the notes within that scale, begin experimenting with short, simple phrases. Play around with the order and rhythm of the notes, and try to create phrases that feel musical. Focus on making each note sound clean and resonant.

As you get more comfortable, start incorporating more complex techniques, such as slides, trills, or vibrato, to add emotion and depth to your melodies. Don't be afraid to experiment with different rhythms, as the Oud can handle a wide range of time signatures, from slow, meditative rhythms to fast, lively patterns.

Begin by composing small, repetitive phrases that you can build upon. As you grow more confident, try to expand your melodies into longer compositions. The beauty of the Oud lies in its capacity for expression, and with practice, you'll be able to convey a wide range of emotions through your playing.

With consistent practice and an understanding of traditional techniques, finger placement, and scale systems, you'll be well on your way to mastering the Oud and creating your own musical journey.

CHAPTER FOUR
Mastering the Essential Oud Skills

The Oud is a fascinating instrument, deeply ingrained in the musical traditions of the Middle East and North Africa. To truly master the Oud, it's essential to understand both the foundational techniques and the cultural nuances that contribute to its unique sound. Whether you're a beginner or an intermediate player, mastering the essential Oud skills is key to becoming proficient and expressive on the instrument.

One of the first steps in learning the Oud is ensuring proper hand positioning. Your left hand should be relaxed, with your fingers arching over the fretboard to allow for clean and precise note production. Pay attention to finger placement, making sure your fingers press down firmly without being tense. On the right hand, the traditional plectrum (referred to as the "risha") is held delicately, allowing for fluid and controlled plucking. Consistent practice will help develop muscle memory, making playing more natural and intuitive.

Plucking with the right hand is crucial in producing the Oud's distinctive sound. Begin by practicing basic plucking motions, gradually increasing speed while maintaining control. Focus on producing clear, even tones without unnecessary noise. The Oud's unique sound is a result of a smooth and controlled plucking technique. Once you're comfortable, experiment with different plucking dynamics, such as soft and loud strokes, to add depth and emotion to your playing.

The left hand must develop strong, independent fingers that can move freely and cleanly across the fretboard. This requires patience and practice, as your fingers need to press each string in a precise manner without muting adjacent strings. Start by practicing scales and simple melodies, ensuring that each note rings out clearly. Over time, you can increase the complexity of the exercises to build more dexterity.

To truly master the Oud, developing your ear is as important as building technique. Being able to identify intervals, melodies, and rhythms will enhance your ability to play by ear and interpret music intuitively. Start by listening to traditional Oud music and trying to play along with recordings. This will help you better understand the unique tonal qualities of the instrument and the subtleties of its performance.

Advanced Techniques: Tremolo, Sliding, and Ornamentation

Once you've established the basics of playing the Oud, it's time to dive into more advanced techniques that will give your playing more depth and character. The techniques of tremolo, sliding, and ornamentation are what separate good Oud players from great ones. Mastering these advanced techniques will allow you to play more expressively and create a richer musical experience.

1. Tremolo: Creating Rich, Sustained Sounds

Tremolo is one of the most powerful techniques in Oud playing. It involves the rapid, repeated movement of the right hand to create a continuous, sustained sound. To master tremolo, begin by practicing slow, controlled movements of the plectrum. As you get more comfortable, increase the speed while maintaining precision. The key is to create a smooth, even tremolo that sounds fluid and connected, almost like a vocal vibrato.

2. Sliding: Smooth Transitions Between Notes

Sliding is an essential technique for adding expression to your playing. It involves shifting smoothly from one note to another, either from a higher or lower pitch. To practice sliding, start with two notes on adjacent frets and slide between them, ensuring that the transition is seamless. This technique is often used to emphasize certain melodic phrases or to create a sense of tension and release. With time, you can experiment with sliding across multiple frets, creating more complex musical phrases.

3. Ornamentation: Adding Subtle Flourishes

Ornamentation refers to the decorative embellishments added to a melody, such as trills, grace notes, and mordents. These subtle touches elevate the overall expression of the music, adding complexity and nuance to your performance. Start by learning basic ornaments and incorporating them into your scales and exercises. As you grow more comfortable with ornamentation, you can begin to incorporate them into your improvisations, adding personal flair to your playing.

Practice Tips for Improving Finger Dexterity and Speed

As with any musical instrument, developing speed and dexterity on the Oud requires consistent and mindful practice. However, it's not just about playing fast—it's about playing cleanly and with precision. Here are some tips to help you build finger dexterity and speed on the Oud.

1. Slow and Steady Wins the Race

When working on increasing speed, always begin by playing slowly and with accuracy. This will help you focus on clean technique and avoid ingraining bad habits. Gradually increase the tempo as you gain confidence, but never sacrifice precision for speed. Using a metronome is invaluable for tracking your progress and ensuring that you maintain proper timing.

2. Finger Independence Exercises

To increase dexterity, work on exercises that challenge the independence of each finger. For example, practice scales, arpeggios, and chromatic exercises while consciously making each finger move independently. Over time, you'll notice an improvement in both your speed and precision as each finger gains strength and coordination.

3. Focus on Left-Hand Movement

While the right hand is important for plucking, the left hand is responsible for pressing the strings and shaping the notes. To develop speed and control, incorporate exercises that focus on rapid finger movement across the fretboard. Start with simple scale patterns, ensuring that each note is clean and distinct. As you progress, increase the difficulty of your exercises by adding more complex passages or increasing the tempo.

4. Alternate Picking for Speed

Another technique to improve speed is alternate picking with the right hand. This involves alternating between upstrokes and downstrokes rather than using only one direction. By mastering alternate picking, you'll be able to play faster without tiring your hand out.

Developing a Strong Sense of Rhythm and Timing

Rhythm and timing are foundational elements of music, and they are particularly important for Oud players. The Oud is often used to accompany vocal performances or other instruments in traditional ensembles, making it crucial for you to develop a strong sense of rhythm.

1. Understanding the Rhythmic Structure

Oud music is based on intricate rhythmic patterns, often referred to as "iqa'at." These rhythms form the backbone of the music and dictate the pacing of the melody. Begin by learning the common iqa'at used in traditional Oud music, such as the 4/4 "maqsoum" or the 6/8 "sa'idi." Practice clapping along to recordings or with a metronome set to the iqa'at of your choice to internalize the rhythm.

2. Playing with a Metronome

A metronome is an essential tool for any musician. It helps keep your timing consistent and accurate. Practice playing along with the metronome, starting slow and gradually increasing the tempo. Focus on staying in time with each beat and subdividing the rhythm into smaller units, such as eighth or sixteenth notes, to improve your precision.

3. Playing Along with Other Musicians

Once you've developed a solid rhythm foundation, playing with other musicians is an excellent way to hone your timing. Whether it's a duet with another Oud player or playing in an ensemble, collaborating with others will push you to stay in time while also responding to the musical cues around you. This real-world practice is invaluable for improving your rhythmic accuracy.

Understanding Oud Notation and Music Theory Basics

Understanding the theory behind the music you play is crucial for a deeper connection with the Oud. Music theory is the language of music, and learning the fundamentals will give you a clearer understanding of how music works, allowing you to be more creative and confident in your playing.

1. Oud Tuning and Scales

The Oud is typically tuned in fourths and fifths, much like a violin or a lute. Learning the tuning system will help you navigate the fretboard more easily. Begin by learning the basic scales used in Oud music, including the Maqam system, which is central to Middle Eastern music. The Maqam system is similar to Western scales but uses microtones, adding a unique flavor to the music.

2. Learning Intervals and Chords

Understanding intervals and chords will help you create harmony and structure in your playing. The Oud, like many string instruments, can be used to play both melody and accompaniment. Practice learning intervals (such as thirds and fifths) and basic chord structures to enrich your playing. While the Oud is not traditionally used for chordal accompaniment in the same way as a guitar, knowing how to build and identify intervals will allow you to create fuller, more complex melodies.

3. Sight-Reading and Notation

Being able to read and write Oud music notation is an important skill for advancing as a musician. Although the Oud has a slightly different notation system than Western music (often using Arabic script or simplified notation), understanding these symbols will allow you to read traditional compositions. Start by learning the basics of Oud notation, such as note values, rests, and articulation marks, and practice sight-reading simple pieces of music.

Exercises for Improving Your Playing Speed and Accuracy

Improving your speed and accuracy on the Oud requires targeted exercises that focus on building both physical skills and mental discipline.

1. Chromatic Scales

Chromatic scales are great for building finger independence and improving your dexterity. Practice playing chromatic scales up and down the fretboard, using alternate picking and focusing on smooth transitions between notes. This exercise will also help you develop a better understanding of the fretboard and improve your speed over time.

2. Arpeggio Patterns

Arpeggios, or broken chords, are fundamental for both solo and accompaniment playing. Practice playing arpeggios in various patterns and positions on the fretboard. Start slow and increase speed as you become more comfortable. Arpeggios help with finger coordination, accuracy, and left-hand strength.

3. Double Stops and Trills

Double stops involve playing two strings simultaneously, and trills involve rapidly alternating between two notes. Both of these exercises will improve your finger strength, coordination, and overall precision. Try playing double stops and trills in different positions on the fretboard, gradually increasing speed while maintaining clarity in each note.

By consistently practicing these skills, techniques, and exercises, you'll gradually develop a strong foundation in Oud playing, progressing from a beginner to an advanced player. Whether you're looking to master intricate ornamentations or simply improve your rhythm and timing, focused practice and dedication will help you achieve your musical goals.

CHAPTER FIVE
Turning Your Oud Passion into a Profitable Business

If you're passionate about playing the oud, turning that passion into a profitable business may seem daunting at first, but with the right approach, it can be a rewarding journey. The oud, with its rich history and unique sound, is a valuable instrument in many musical traditions. It's not just about playing for personal fulfillment; it's about creating value that others are willing to pay for.

The first step in turning your oud passion into a business is to identify the different income streams that are available to you. Whether it's through teaching, performing, recording, or creating content, there are multiple avenues to generate income. The key is to understand your strengths, your market, and how you can provide value to your audience.

It's also important to think about the long-term sustainability of your business. Building a brand, staying consistent, and adapting to changes in the industry will all play key roles in growing your oud music business. This could mean transitioning from a hobbyist musician to a full-fledged professional or simply earning supplemental income while keeping music at the center of your life.

Identifying Opportunities for Profit Through Oud Playing

The first step in making a profit as an oud player is identifying the opportunities available to you. These opportunities vary based on your skills, your audience, and your market, but some common options include:

1. **Teaching Oud**: Many aspiring musicians want to learn how to play the oud but don't know where to start. If you have a solid understanding of the instrument, offering lessons (either in-person or online) can be a profitable venture. You can teach beginner, intermediate, and advanced students, tailoring your lessons to their individual needs. There are even opportunities to teach the oud on music education platforms that reach a wider global audience.
2. **Live Performances**: Performing live is one of the most traditional and profitable ways of making money as an oud player. This could involve performing at cultural events, weddings, concerts, or festivals. If you're able to perform a wide range of genres or specialize in a particular style, you can appeal to diverse audiences and secure paid gigs.
3. **Recording and Selling Music**: Recording your music and selling it through platforms

like Spotify, Apple Music, or Bandcamp can be a great way to reach a global audience. The music industry is increasingly digital, and you don't need a record label to get your music out there. You can also sell physical copies of your music, such as CDs or vinyl records, at performances or online.

4. **Collaborations**: The oud is a unique instrument that pairs well with a variety of musical genres. By collaborating with other musicians—whether they're singers, instrumentalists, or bands—you can expand your reach and tap into new markets. These collaborations can also lead to higher-paying performance opportunities.

5. **Creating Educational Content**: Another profitable opportunity is creating online tutorials, courses, or content to teach others how to play the oud. With the increasing popularity of online learning, there's a growing demand for instructional videos or

written materials that help others learn the instrument.

Building an Online Presence for Your Music Business

In today's digital age, having an online presence is non-negotiable if you want to grow your oud music business. Your online presence serves as the first point of contact for many potential clients, fans, and collaborators. A well-maintained online presence allows you to build credibility, promote your work, and expand your audience. Here's how you can effectively build an online presence for your oud business:

1. **Create a Professional Website**: Your website should be the hub of your online presence. It's where potential clients can find all the information they need about your services, your music, and how to contact

you. Your website should include a portfolio of your work, your bio, performance schedule, and a blog where you can share your thoughts on music and the oud.

2. **Social Media Engagement**: Platforms like Instagram, YouTube, and Facebook are perfect for musicians. On Instagram, you can post short clips of your performances or practice sessions. YouTube is ideal for longer videos, such as full performances, tutorials, or behind-the-scenes content. Facebook allows you to connect with fans and share events or upcoming gigs. Consistency is key in social media—keep your audience engaged with regular updates and interactive content.

3. **Email Newsletter**: A well-managed email list can be a valuable tool for promoting your music business. You can send updates about upcoming performances, new music releases, or special offers for private lessons. Offering a free music lesson, a

downloadable song, or an exclusive video in exchange for signing up can encourage people to subscribe.

4. **SEO and Content Marketing**: To make sure people can find you online, it's essential to work on your search engine optimization (SEO). This includes using relevant keywords, optimizing your website's structure, and creating valuable content that helps your audience. For example, writing blog posts on topics like "How to Play the Oud" or "The History of the Oud" can attract traffic to your site.

How to Create a Professional Portfolio as an Oud Musician

Creating a professional portfolio is essential for showcasing your skills and experience as an oud musician. A portfolio serves as your visual and auditory resume, helping you attract clients, collaborators, and performance opportunities. Here's how you can create a compelling portfolio:

1. **Record Your Best Performances**: The cornerstone of your portfolio should be recordings of your best performances. Include a variety of styles or compositions that demonstrate your versatility on the oud. If possible, get your performances professionally recorded to ensure high-quality sound and video.
2. **Showcase Your Music Skills**: Your portfolio should not only showcase your performances but also highlight your technical abilities. Include examples of your compositions, improvisation skills, and any other relevant musical talent. If you teach oud music, include testimonials from students who can attest to your teaching style and effectiveness.
3. **Create a Biography**: Your bio should include your background as an oud musician, your musical influences, any

formal education or training, and notable performances or collaborations. This helps potential clients or collaborators understand your experience and expertise.

4. **Include Client Testimonials**: If you've performed at events, taught lessons, or worked with other musicians, include testimonials in your portfolio. A positive recommendation from a satisfied client can go a long way in establishing your credibility.

5. **Make It Easy to Navigate**: Ensure that your portfolio is easy to access and navigate, whether it's a website or a physical portfolio. Make sure your contact information is prominently displayed, and include links to your social media or music platforms for easy access to your content.

Monetizing Your Skills: Teaching, Performing, and Recording

Once you've honed your skills on the oud, there are several ways you can monetize them. The key is to diversify your income streams and explore various avenues for making money as a musician.

1. **Teaching**: Offering private lessons, whether in-person or online, is a steady way to generate income. You can offer one-on-one lessons or group classes for beginners or advanced students. You can also expand your reach by offering courses through online platforms like Udemy or Skillshare.
2. **Performing**: Performing live remains one of the most direct ways to make money as an oud musician. Look for opportunities at local venues, cultural events, and weddings. Don't forget to consider virtual performances—many artists have made a

name for themselves by streaming live performances online.

3. **Recording**: Recording and selling your music digitally or physically allows you to earn money each time someone listens to your music. Digital platforms like iTunes, Spotify, and YouTube can help distribute your music worldwide. Consider releasing singles or albums and promoting them through your online channels.

4. **Composing for Film, TV, and Commercials**: If you're skilled at composing music, consider offering your services to filmmakers, advertising agencies, or production companies. The unique sound of the oud can bring a distinct flavor to any project, and composers are often sought after for original, authentic sounds.

Networking Tips and How to Grow Your Business Locally and Globally

Networking is essential for any musician looking to grow their business. Building connections within your local music scene as well as the global community can help you find new performance opportunities, collaborators, and clients. Here are some tips on how to network effectively:

1. **Attend Local Events and Festivals**: One of the best ways to grow your network is by attending live music events, festivals, or local meetups. This is where you can meet fellow musicians, event organizers, and potential clients. Don't be afraid to introduce yourself and let others know about your skills.
2. **Collaborate with Other Musicians**: Collaboration is a great way to expand your

reach. By working with musicians from different backgrounds or genres, you can expose your music to new audiences. Collaborations often lead to joint performances, recordings, and cross-promotion.

3. **Join Online Communities**: There are countless online communities for musicians, both general and niche. Platforms like Facebook Groups, Reddit, and even specific forums for oud musicians can help you find like-minded individuals, share tips, and discover new opportunities.

4. **Use Social Media to Connect Globally**: Social media platforms provide an easy way to connect with musicians and music enthusiasts worldwide. Reach out to fellow oud players, influencers, and music producers to explore collaborative opportunities. Share your performances and join discussions to engage with a global community.

5. **Build Relationships with Event Organizers**: Building relationships with event organizers or venue owners can provide long-term opportunities for paid performances. Let them know about your availability and the types of performances you offer, and always follow up after events to maintain the connection.

By applying these strategies and consistently working on building your brand, you can grow your oud music business both locally and globally. Networking, combined with a strong online presence and diverse income streams, can help turn your oud passion into a sustainable and profitable business.

CHAPTER SIX
Common Challenges and How to Overcome Them

Learning to play the oud can be both an exciting and challenging journey. As with any musical instrument, there are certain obstacles that students and players of all levels often face. From developing finger techniques to dealing with performance anxiety, understanding these challenges and finding ways to overcome them is key to making progress. Below, we explore common difficulties and provide practical solutions for each, so you can continue your oud-playing journey with confidence.

1. Difficulty in Mastering Finger Techniques and Overcoming Hand Fatigue

The Challenge:

One of the first challenges you will encounter when playing the oud is mastering the finger techniques. The oud requires precise finger placements on the fretboard, and for beginners, this can cause discomfort and hand fatigue. The tension and coordination between the fingers can make it difficult to form the right chords or to play fluidly, especially if you're not accustomed to the movement or the pressure needed.

Overcoming It:

- **Build Finger Strength Gradually**: Start by practicing simple finger exercises to build strength and dexterity. Focus on each finger independently, playing scales and arpeggios slowly and gradually increasing the speed. This will help develop the muscles in your fingers and reduce fatigue over time.

- **Proper Hand Positioning**: Pay close attention to the position of your wrist, fingers, and forearm. A relaxed wrist and hand will help prevent tension. Position your hand at an angle that allows your fingers to press down on the strings comfortably, avoiding unnecessary strain.
- **Take Breaks and Stretch**: Hand fatigue is common, especially in the beginning stages. To prevent overuse injuries, take regular breaks during practice sessions. Stretch your fingers and wrists before and after playing to release any tension. This will not only help your fingers but also keep your arms and shoulders relaxed.
- **Use a Supportive Posture**: Make sure you are sitting or standing with good posture. Sitting in a way that supports your back,

neck, and arms can reduce the strain on your hands. If you're finding it difficult to maintain a steady position, consider using a footstool or cushion to elevate your leg, supporting your body during practice.

2. How to Deal with Slow Progress and Stay Motivated

The Challenge:

One of the hardest parts of learning a musical instrument is dealing with slow progress. You might feel frustrated when your playing doesn't improve as quickly as you'd like, or when your skills plateau. It's natural to experience moments of self-doubt, especially in the early stages of learning the oud.

Overcoming It:

- **Set Realistic Goals**: Break down your learning process into smaller, achievable goals. For example, rather than aiming to learn a whole song in one week, focus on mastering a few chords or a short melody. Celebrate the small victories along the way, as each step forward is an accomplishment.

- **Embrace Consistent Practice**: Practice doesn't always have to be lengthy or intense. Even short, focused sessions can yield significant results over time. Consistency is key—make practicing a daily habit, even if it's just for 15-30 minutes. Over time, this regular practice will lead to steady improvement.
- **Stay Inspired by Your Love for the Music**: Keep reminding yourself why you started learning the oud in the first place. Connect with the music you're playing, listen to recordings, or watch performances to reignite your passion. This can serve as a powerful motivator when progress feels slow.

- **Be Patient with Yourself**: Learning a new instrument is a long-term process. Understand that there will be ups and downs. If you encounter obstacles, take a step back and focus on the joy of playing rather than just the results. Remember, every practice session contributes to your improvement.

3. Common Mistakes in Playing and How to Correct Them

The Challenge:

As with any instrument, beginners often make certain mistakes that can hinder progress. In the case of the oud, common mistakes include improper finger placement, poor strumming techniques, and rushing through songs without paying attention to detail.

Overcoming It:

- **Improper Finger Placement**: Ensure that your fingers are pressing down on the strings with enough force to produce a clean sound. Avoid pressing too hard, which can mute the notes, or too softly, which may result in buzzing sounds. Pay attention to your finger placement, aiming for just behind the fret to produce a clear note.
- **Strumming Techniques**: The oud's unique sound comes from its distinct strumming pattern. Many beginners rush through their strumming or fail to maintain a steady rhythm. Slow down and practice the strumming patterns, paying attention to the dynamics and accents. Start with basic down-strokes and up-strokes, then gradually move to more complex techniques like using a plectrum.
- **Not Listening to Your Sound**: One key mistake is not paying attention to how the notes sound as you play. Always listen

carefully for inconsistencies, buzzing, or muted sounds. If something sounds off, stop and figure out what might be causing the issue—whether it's finger placement, string pressure, or posture.
- **Skipping the Basics**: It can be tempting to jump straight into playing your favorite songs, but building a solid foundation is essential. Spend time mastering scales, basic rhythms, and finger exercises. This solid groundwork will improve your playing in the long run and make learning more complex pieces easier.

4. Finding the Right Resources and Learning Tools

The Challenge:

In today's digital world, there's an overwhelming amount of resources available for learning the oud, and it can be difficult to find the best ones. Whether it's finding the right tutorials, sheet music, or video lessons, you need resources that are effective and suit your learning style.

Overcoming It:

- **Choose Quality Learning Platforms**: Look for trusted websites and online courses that offer structured lessons. Sites like Udemy, YouTube channels dedicated to oud tutorials, or online academies can provide high-quality, step-by-step instruction. Make sure to read reviews or recommendations to ensure the resources are credible.
- **Books and Sheet Music**: Invest in a good oud method book that explains techniques, music theory, and provides practice exercises. These books often include finger exercises, basic songs, and rhythm practice. Additionally, learning to read music notation for oud-specific songs will be beneficial.

- **Private Lessons or Mentorship**: If you're finding it difficult to navigate resources on your own, consider taking private lessons.
- A qualified teacher can give you personalized feedback and tailor lessons to your needs. Having someone guide you through the learning process can be invaluable.
- **Join a Community**: Learning the oud can feel isolating at times, but connecting with other players can help you stay motivated. Join online communities, forums, or local oud clubs to share experiences, get advice, and learn from others. Listening to and learning from more experienced players will enhance your playing.

5. Dealing with Performance Anxiety and Gaining Confidence on Stage

The Challenge:

Many oud players struggle with performance anxiety when they have to play in front of others. Whether it's in front of friends, family, or a live audience, the fear of making mistakes or not playing perfectly can be overwhelming.

Overcoming It:

- **Preparation is Key**: One of the best ways to build confidence is by being well-prepared. Practice your pieces until you can play them confidently without looking at your hands. The more familiar you are with your music, the less you'll worry about mistakes on stage.

- **Start Small**: If performing in front of a large audience feels daunting, start by playing for just one or two people. Gradually increase the number of listeners as you become more comfortable with the experience. The more you perform, the more natural it will feel.
- **Use Relaxation Techniques**: Deep breathing, meditation, or visualization techniques can help calm your nerves before a performance.
- Take a few minutes to center yourself, clear your mind, and focus on the music rather than the audience's expectations.
- **Embrace Imperfection**: It's important to realize that no performance is ever perfect, and mistakes are a natural part of live music. If you make an error during a performance, continue playing without dwelling on it. The audience is often more focused on the overall experience than on small mistakes.
- **Gain Experience**: The more you perform, the less anxiety you'll feel over time. Even

practicing in front of a mirror or recording your practice sessions can help build comfort with performing. The goal is to make performing a natural extension of your practice, rather than something that causes stress.

By addressing these challenges head-on and utilizing these solutions, you will be able to overcome obstacles more effectively and progress faster in your oud playing journey.

Remember that every musician faces difficulties along the way, but with the right mindset, patience, and perseverance, you can overcome them and continue to grow as a skilled oud player.

CHAPTER SEVEN
Long-Term Success in Oud Playing and Business

Achieving long-term success in playing the Oud, whether as a musician or a businessperson, requires a blend of musical talent, perseverance, and strategic planning. The Oud is a traditional instrument with rich cultural significance, but succeeding with it in today's competitive music landscape requires more than just technical proficiency. It involves cultivating a unique sound, expanding your reach, and building a sustainable career both on and off the stage. Here are some essential elements for ensuring long-term success in Oud playing and business.

Setting Long-Term Goals for Your Musical and Business Growth

One of the cornerstones of success in any field is the establishment of clear, actionable long-term goals. For Oud players, this involves creating a roadmap for both musical mastery and business development. Setting specific, measurable, attainable, relevant, and time-bound (SMART) goals allows you to track your progress and stay motivated.

- **Musical Growth**: Define where you want to be with your playing in five, ten, or even twenty years. Do you wish to master a particular style or genre of Oud music? Are you aspiring to collaborate with other musicians, perform in international venues, or perhaps create a legacy through educational content?

- **Business Development**: In terms of the business side of Oud playing, your goals might involve expanding your brand, increasing your social media presence, creating merchandise, or monetizing your performances through various channels such as live events, streaming platforms, or even teaching online lessons.

Setting realistic benchmarks for both your artistry and entrepreneurial activities ensures you're consistently working towards something, keeping you focused on long-term success rather than quick, short-lived victories.

Continuous Improvement: Ongoing Practice and Education

In any musical discipline, mastery is a lifelong journey. The Oud, with its complex techniques and rich history, requires ongoing practice and education. As a player, this means committing to constant improvement, whether through self-study, formal lessons, or peer interaction.

- **Practice**: The foundation of musical growth is regular, disciplined practice. As an Oud player, it's essential to set aside time every day to refine your technique, learn new pieces, and experiment with different styles. Consistency is key. Even on days when progress seems slow, your dedication to practicing will compound over time, and your skills will steadily improve.
- **Education**: Learning never stops. Take advantage of online resources, attend workshops, participate in masterclasses, or learn from other Oud players. Engage with a teacher who can offer personalized feedback and help you break through plateaus. Additionally, broadening your musical knowledge, such as understanding music theory or the history of Oud music, will

deepen your appreciation for the instrument and enhance your performance.

By committing to continuous improvement, you ensure that your playing remains fresh and that you stay relevant in the evolving music industry.

How to Evolve Your Unique Style as an Oud Player

Developing a distinctive style is crucial for standing out in the competitive music world. Your style as an Oud player is what will make you recognizable and memorable to your audience. Evolving your unique sound involves a mix of creativity, influences, and practice.

- **Experimentation**: To find your voice, experiment with various genres and techniques. While traditional Oud music is rich and beautiful, don't be afraid to blend different styles—whether that's jazz, classical, or even fusion with other instruments. By doing this, you'll start to discover what resonates with your personal taste and the sound you want to create.

- **Influences**: Take time to listen to and analyze different Oud players, both historical and contemporary. Identify what elements you admire in their playing and see if you can incorporate similar techniques into your own playing. This will allow you to build upon the traditions while adding your own flair to the instrument.
- **Improvisation**: The Oud is an instrument known for its emotive power and versatility, especially in improvisation. By honing your improvisational skills, you can bring a level of personal expression to your performances that will set you apart from others. Take inspiration from different musical forms and apply them to your own interpretation of Oud music.

In time, your unique style will evolve naturally as you continue to experiment, refine, and express yourself through the Oud.

Building a Loyal Fan Base and Growing Your Audience

A successful career in music requires more than just great playing—it's about connecting with your audience and building a community around your music. A loyal fan base is not something that happens overnight, but with dedication, it's entirely achievable.

- **Social Media and Digital Platforms**: In today's digital age, social media is a powerful tool for connecting with fans and sharing your journey as an Oud player. Platforms like Instagram, YouTube, and Facebook allow you to showcase your talent, share your process, and engage with your audience in real time. Regular content updates, whether through performances, behind-the-scenes footage, or personal stories, keep your audience engaged and excited about your work.

- **Live Performances**: There's no substitute for live interaction. Performing live not only helps you connect with your current fans, but it also exposes you to new audiences. Play at local events, cultural festivals, and collaborate with other musicians to increase your exposure. Over time, your reputation will grow, and word of mouth will help you attract more fans.
- **Engagement**: To build loyalty, make sure to engage with your audience regularly. Respond to comments, acknowledge support, and even involve fans in decisions (such as letting them vote on which song you should play next). Creating a relationship with your listeners makes them feel valued, fostering long-term loyalty.

By leveraging the power of online platforms and live performances, you can build a dedicated following that supports your work and encourages your growth.

Sustainable Ways to Make a Career in Music with Oud Playing

Turning your passion for the Oud into a sustainable career requires a strategic approach to music business management. There are several ways to ensure that your career with the Oud remains financially stable and fulfilling over the long term.

- **Diversify Your Income Streams**: Relying solely on one revenue source can be risky. In addition to performing live, consider offering online lessons for aspiring Oud players. Creating educational content, such as tutorials or courses, can help you reach a global audience and generate steady income. Moreover, collaborating with other musicians, recording albums, or licensing your music for use in film, TV, or commercials can provide additional streams of revenue.

- **Merchandising**: Another avenue for financial growth is through merchandise. Offer branded products like T-shirts, posters, or even Oud accessories. These items can be sold at your performances or online, creating a secondary source of income while also promoting your brand.
- **Grants and Sponsorships**: As a professional Oud player, you may be eligible for grants or sponsorships that support your work. Many cultural organizations and music foundations offer funding for artists to produce albums, tour, or create educational programs. Building relationships with sponsors or music industry partners can also provide opportunities for cross-promotion and mutual support.

- **Networking and Collaborations**: Networking is a key aspect of sustaining a career in music. Collaborate with other musicians and producers to expand your reach and increase your credibility within the music industry. Working with people who share similar musical interests will not only help you grow but also open doors to new opportunities.

Building a sustainable career with the Oud involves diversifying your income, making strategic business decisions, and continuously looking for ways to expand your brand and reach. By doing so, you can ensure long-term success as both a musician and a businessperson.

Conclusion: The Path to Mastery and Profit

Mastering the Oud is not simply about learning to play an instrument; it's about embarking on a transformative journey. Whether you're a beginner or an experienced player, there are always new levels to reach. The Oud is an intricate instrument that requires both patience and dedication, but once you master it, the rewards are invaluable—not just in terms of musical proficiency but also in personal fulfillment and career opportunities.

By honing your skills, you not only enhance your musicality but open doors to potential business opportunities as well. From live performances to teaching, recording, and even selling your music, the Oud can be a lucrative source of both personal expression and financial success. The path to mastery is not always straightforward, but each step forward brings its own sense of achievement and potential. Reflecting on your progress regularly allows you to assess where you've come from, understand your strengths, and see where there's room for growth.

This chapter will guide you on how to move forward with your Oud playing journey while ensuring that your efforts translate into success—both in your music and your career.

Reflecting on Your Progress and Future Goals in Oud Playing

As you look back on your journey with the Oud, it's essential to take stock of the progress you've made. Reflecting on where you started, the challenges you've faced, and the skills you've developed gives you a deeper sense of accomplishment. Reflecting also allows you to measure how much further you have to go and can reignite the motivation you need to push yourself further.

Start by considering your technical skills—how comfortable are you with different scales, ornamentations, and rhythms? Have you developed a sense of musicality that lets you express your emotions through your playing?

Equally important is understanding how your musical abilities can help shape your future. Whether it's aiming to perform at larger venues, recording your own compositions, or even teaching others, setting clear, actionable goals will keep you focused. These goals might range from small steps, like mastering a specific piece, to long-term objectives, like building a career as a full-time musician.

The Importance of Persistence and Dedication in Both Music and Business

Mastery of the Oud, or any musical instrument, is not attained overnight. It requires years of consistent practice, overcoming frustration, and learning from failures. The same principle applies to turning your passion for Oud into a successful career.

Musicians often face obstacles in their journey, whether it's difficulty mastering a technique, dealing with stage fright, or navigating the competitive music industry. But perseverance is key. In both music and business, your dedication is what will keep you moving forward, even when things get tough.

In the business side of things, persistence and dedication can mean continuously seeking performance opportunities, marketing yourself effectively, and learning how to manage finances and negotiations. For example, many musicians face the challenge of creating a profitable income from their passion, but it is possible through determination. Finding avenues for monetizing your music, like teaching, selling recordings, or performing at events, will be part of the long journey to success.

But most importantly, never lose sight of your original love for playing the Oud. Let it fuel your persistence and dedication. The journey will have its highs and lows, but staying focused on both the music and business side will allow you to achieve both artistic and financial success.

How to Stay Connected with the Oud Community and Continue Learning

The Oud community is vast, diverse, and full of opportunities to learn from others. Staying connected to this community will not only enrich your musical journey but will also provide valuable support and networking opportunities that can help you in your career.

Attend Oud festivals, workshops, and concerts whenever you can. These events offer opportunities to learn from master players, exchange ideas with fellow musicians, and gain exposure. The online world also offers a wealth of resources. Platforms like YouTube, social media groups, and music forums are excellent ways to keep learning and stay updated with the latest trends, techniques, and innovations in Oud playing.

You might also consider working with a mentor or teacher who can guide you and provide constructive feedback. Many successful musicians have reached where they are today because they never stopped learning from others, whether through private lessons, collaborations, or even attending open jams.

Moreover, don't be afraid to share your own experiences and knowledge. By teaching others, you not only solidify your own understanding but also create connections that can lead to new opportunities in your career.

Encouragement to Pursue Your Passion and Turn It Into a Successful Career

It's one thing to play music for fun; it's another to turn it into a successful career. The path to doing so is rarely linear, and it involves a combination of talent, strategic thinking, networking, and persistence.

If you truly want to turn your passion for the Oud into a profession, start by envisioning what success looks like for you. Does it involve performing for large audiences? Or perhaps you want to record and sell albums? Maybe your dream is to teach others how to play the Oud. Whatever it may be, it's important to set clear goals and create a roadmap to achieve them.

In the world of music, success doesn't always come in the form of instant recognition. It's often the result of building a reputation slowly and steadily over time. Consistent practice, strong networking, and embracing every opportunity to learn and perform will gradually help you gain the experience and skills necessary to achieve your dreams.

Stay passionate and keep pushing yourself to evolve both as a musician and an entrepreneur.

This path may take time, but by staying focused, you'll be able to transform your love for the Oud into a sustainable and rewarding career.

Final Words of Motivation to Keep Going on Your Journey of Mastery

No matter where you are on your journey of mastering the Oud, remember that every step counts. The road may seem long, but it's also rich with learning, growth, and self-discovery. The challenges you face today will only make you stronger tomorrow.

Each time you pick up your Oud, whether for practice or performance, you're shaping your future. You're becoming not only a better musician but a more disciplined and determined individual. The rewards of mastery are worth the effort, and the joy of connecting deeply with your instrument and your audience is irreplaceable.

Keep pushing forward, even on the days when it feels difficult. The path may seem overwhelming at times, but the key is to break it down into manageable steps. Whether you're working towards your first paid performance or planning your debut album, always remember that your passion is your strongest asset.

So, stay focused on your goals, keep improving, and never give up on your dream. The journey to mastery is ongoing, and your potential is limitless. Keep playing, keep learning, and above all, keep believing in yourself. Your dedication to the Oud will not only elevate your musical abilities but will also help you create a meaningful, lasting career that resonates with others. Keep going—you're on the path to greatness!

THE END

Manufactured by Amazon.ca
Acheson, AB